WORDS
From the
HEART

A Collection of Poetry

And Short Prose

WORDS
From the
HEART

by Alberta Harvey

Publishing

Copyright © 2011

Revision ... 2013

By Alberta Harvey 24510-Harv

ISBN: Softcover 978-0- 9840260-3-6

All rights reserved. No part of this book may be reproduced or utilized in any form by any means, electronic or mechanical, including photocopying, recording, or by any information storage or retrieval system, without permission in writing from the publisher.

This book was printed in the United States of America. To order additional copies of this book contact: Unique Euphony Publishing Group

706-577-3197

www.uniqueeuphony.com

uniqueeuphonypublishing@inbox.com

Layout Design by Barbara Pierce
Cover Design by Kirk Knox

Preface

My dream has been to write and publish my books. That dream came true with the publication of my first book *Our Roots;* June 2006. The dream continued as I published my second book; My *Thoughts on Paper;* July 2010 and my dream continues as I publish my third book; Words *from the Heart; November* 2011.

My passion for writing expands my world, increases my awareness, and lets me share my journey in life with others…

Table of Contents

Faith, Family, Friends

Church   5

We Are   6

Faith   7

No Place to Call Home   8

In This Life   9

Her Book   10

My Friend   11

G.E.D.   12

My Life's Work   13

This Life   14

Heart, Hope, Hands

Our Culture   17

Our Hands   18

Our Family   19

A Daughter   20

Thanksgiving   21

Christmas   22

Valentine   23

A Rose   24

Winter   25

Spring   26

Summer   27

Autumn   28

Live, Love, Laugh

This Day   31

Blue Sky   32

Clouds   33

The Color Blue   34

The Cornfields   35

Colors You Feel   36

Feelings That Touch You   37

Laughter   38

My First Trip   40

My Dream   42

Hatha Yoga   45

Why I Write   47

A Poem   *48*

Poems of Life

Shape   *49*

What is Love   *50*

A Mother   *51*

Empowering   *52*

Wisdom   *53*

Pray   *54*

Heavenly   *55*

Someone Knows My Name   *56*

What's in a name?   *57*
Alberta   *58*
James   *59*
Virginia   *60*
Teddy   *61*
Mary   *62*
Della   *63*

About the Author   *64*

F aith

F amily

F riend

Church

C Coming together to worship
H Hands held high in praise
U Unified by their faith
R Revealing their trust in God
C Confident in His Grace and Mercy
H Holding on to His eternal love

We Are

Restored from the wages of sin

Enriched by his love

Delivered by his grace and mercy

Engaged in his written word

Enriched by praising his name

Making heaven our goal

Embracing him in our prayers

Devoted to our trust in God

Faith

Faith is a gift

A believe without doubt

A trust without proof

Peace of mind in His love

A joy in a world of sorrow Hope

in His word for internal life His

love is our strength

Go forward in faith

No Place to Call Home

Your home humble as it maybe
It is still home sweet home
Nothing can replace this space
There may be an urge to roam
But you will always want a place to call home

With no place to call home
You feel alone, disserted and afraid
All your days blend into one Your thoughts go around in circles
Time passes oh so slow

You dream about a home
No matter how small
A roof overhead and walls around
A place of your own
There is just no place like home!

In This Life

Love the Lord with all your heart
Listen to His word
Learn to follow His way Look
for love in all you do Leave
the bonds of sin behind Lift
your hands to heaven
Let the lord lead you home.

Her Book

Now take a Look

At the change Bert Took

Her thoughts flowing like a Brook

To fill every page's Nook

With words that would Hook

Emotions with be Shook

When Bert publishers her Book

by Teddy T. Rouse

My Friend

It is good to be free
as I look at the sea

My friends are around
so I rarely frown

I would like to catch a fish
but I don't have a dish

I really miss my special friend
Hope I'll be able to see him again

He really meant a lot to me!

by Katrina Coleman

G.E.D
General Education Diploma

I would like to get my G.E.D

I left school to go to work

I worked hard all my life

Making sure the job was done right I was paid well

and felt good, but later in my life I realize I didn't

get

what I needed to get where I wanted to be

My High School Diploma

A regret expressed…

by Charlie Johnson

My Life's Work

As a cement mason I poured and finish concrete
This process takes a of number of steps
First you set the forms that hold and align the concrete
Then you pour the concrete into the formed area using specialized tools you spread it around The tools are "bull float," broom or stiff-bristled brush or a trowel
Each stool can create a different type of surfaces
You remove the forms

Then you must smooth any rough surfaces that remain
This operation is called finishing

by Charles Johnson

This Life

It is not how long you live
But about how much you give
The more of everything you share
The more you will have to spare
Love is a gift you give away
This act will enrich your life each day
Life is faith, family, and friends

Heart
ope
and

Our Culture

Covering our American and African Heritage

Uniting us in a bond of love and dignity

Lets us use our bonds to build our community

These bonds will let us know who we are and where we are going

Uncovering our talents, knowledge, and faith

Reminding us of our social skills and struggles

Empowering us to live a joyous life!

Our Hands

Can hold the Holy Bible
Clapped to praise His name
Raise high to worship Him
Pressed together in prayer
Join hands together for pray
Hands are shaken in greeting with others
Hands can make a difference, lend a hand
Make the world a better place

My Family

Fun, fighting, and forgiving
They are always there for you

Some have come and some have gone
There are so many wonderful memories

A bond love for family keeps us together
when you have family you are truly blessed

A Daughter

A Daughter brings sunshine to brighten your days

She brings joy through her loving ways

A Daughter is a blessing that comes from above

She is a beautiful treasure to behold

A Daughter is a voice of who you are

Thanksgiving

Thanksgiving is a holiday to be thankful There

may be ham, yams, and black-eyed peas

But having family and friends around you

Is what will make your Thanksgiving

A thankful and Happy Thanksgiving

Christmas Day

Everyone wants to give a gift at Christmas time
Something just right to go under that pine

There is a gift that needs no wrapping to unfold you
can't even buy it with silver or gold

It's the glorious gift of love that crosses my mind

Valentine

You are my Valentine

You bring me joy and happiness

You make my love shine

You are my love

Happy Valentine

A Rose

Of all the flowers I know

A rose says it best

So let your love shine

Through the beauty of a rose

The earth was made with love

From that earth a rose sprang

So give a rose to the one you love

Winter Is

Winter is a white
for the blanket of snow

Winter is icicles
glittering like gold

Winter is a time to
stay indoors

Winter is coziness
as the furnace roars

Winter is a way to
give nature a rest

Winter is so cold
it puts all to a test

Winter's freezing
is a mighty good reason

Winter is followed
by warm spring breezes

Spring Time

Spring is a new beginning

Grass begins to grow

Tree leaves begin to spout

Flowers start to bloom

Birds gather and begin to sing

The rains come to water the new growth

Then the sun begins warming the new life.

Summer Time

Summer is, oh so hot!

Lazy, hazy days a lot

you picnic in the park

Barbecue in the back yard

School is out kids are about

you take time off from your job

Company comes and wears you out

Oh! How I long for autumn

Autumn is what I love most of all

So let the summer fade to fall

Autumn

Nature begins to decline

Grass stops growing

Tree leaves change colors

And fall from the trees

Flowers stop blooming

Birds fly south

Temperature turns cold

LIVE

LOVE

LAUGH

This Day

Day is breaking

Darkness is fading

The sun is shining

The sky is a soft blue

A new day has began

What will this day bring?

Blue Sky

The sky is blue

As far as the eye can see

not a cloud in the sky

The sun is shining

Making the sky

Feel so soft, calm, and peaceful

Only God could make a Universe so perfect

Clouds

Oh so magnificent

Snow white and fluffy

So many different shapes

Floating across the clean blue sky

Only the wind knows their destination

I wish I could leap up there

Sit on their surface and float along with them

So I could see the valleys and hills as the pass beneath me

It would be so peaceful drifting along with the unseen wind.

The Color Blue

Blue is a wonderful color to behold

Weather it is the clear blue sky

Or the rippling waves of the ocean

A Blue Jay soaring through the air

Or a human face with blue eyes

A blue ribbon to announce a baby boy

Or the star studded blue of the American Flag

You can hear, sing, or play the blues

You can wear blue cloths, hat, socks, or shoes

There are the blue uniforms of the Sailor, Airman, and Policeman

You can find many things that are blue; crayon, thread, paint, ink

Blue can be wavy, filled with stars, announce a birth, or show your feelings,

As you probably know by now my favorite color is blue

The Cornfields

You can see their long green stalks spread across the field

All lined up in straight and even rows Their

golden tassels reaching for the sky

Their shaves filled with golden ears of corn

These fields of corn provide food humans and animals

So let their stalks spread across the farm land

So the farmers can harvest this golden crop

Colors you can feel

The warmth of the golden sun

The golden beauty of a sunset

The coldness of the white snow

The white twinkling stars in the night sky

The wetness of the lake's blue water

The soft blue of the clear morning sky

The softness of the green grass

The red and yellow of the autumn leaves

The purple of the bruise on your knee

The purple Irises blooming across the field

Feelings that Touch You

The expression of love
The shouts of joy
The gift of kindness
The pain of rejection
The rage of anger
The hurt of rudeness
The sadness of grief
The fear of how others perceive you
The knowledge that life isn't always fair
The power of faith and the hope of eternal life!

Laugh

Laughter brings the gift of joy

Allowing your body to relax and mind to clear

Unleash yourself and roar with laughter

Giggle, snigger, or chuckle

However you do it the whole body gets involved

Laugh

H happiness is the sunshine on your face

G gaps your belly and roar

U use laughter to brighten your day

A allowing it to spread to those around you

L live, love and laugh

My First Trip

I grew up on a small farm in Sullivan, Indiana and began my travels when I joined the Army 1958. My first trip took me from Sullivan to Indianapolis, to Birmingham, to Anniston, and then to Fort McClellan Army Base in Alabama. When arrived there I had traveled by car, bus, train and a taxi. The taxi ride was the first time I ran into segregation.

    I was with two White girls and we were not able to ride together in the same cab even though we were in the same Army fighting for the same country. This was so upsetting to all three of us we were ready to go back home. We took the separate caps and when we arrived at the barracks we got out of the taxi's and hugged each other before we went into the building.

Once inside we saw the sergeant sitting behind a desk. She immediately told us we could be together on post but not off post. I said to her I can't believe I am here to protect our country's freedom and I don't have that same freedom. The Sergeant did not answer my disbelief she only told us where to go and what we needed to do. I said to myself the road that brought me here was full of bumps, bridges, tunnels, crossroads and red lights so I am going to do my best to overcome the obstacles I see I will be facing in my life's journey.

My Dream Job!

My career changed from nursing to writing, my dream. If you love what you are doing it is not really a job. Putting thoughts on paper is my passion. I love writing for the freedom of a new beginning with each blank page. This challenge expands my world, increases my awareness, and lets me share my journey with others.

Flexibility is what makes the title entrepreneur so rewarding. Thoughts come to you at different times of the day or night so you want to be able to put them on paper. I keep a pen and paper with me at all times. I would not want to forget an idea that came to me and I had not written it down.

I would like to think that my writing will provide information for others that could help them solve problems or make a difference in their lives. The pen has power that can bring a thoughtful moment, hope, sadness, or a good laugh.

I have a home-based business where. I write articles, essays, and poetry. I have published two articles, two essays and two books **"Our Roots"** our family history and genealogy, **"My Thoughts on Paper** a book of poetry and short prose.

Traveling is another thing I love to do. I have traveled a lot in my life and each trip was an adventure. It is not only the places you go but the people you meet. I would like to share these people in a book called **"People Along the Way"**. It is the people you meet that makes traveling such a rewarding experience.

Hatha Yoga

Hatha Yoga is one of my favorite pleasure time activities. It is a combination of body positions, rhythmic breathing, and visual imagery.

I learned about Yoga through my place of employment. It was a six week course and was recommended as a way to reduce stress. I took the course and to this day I continue to practice Yoga.

The exercise tones and rejuvenates my body. The rhythmic breathing renews my thoughts of wellness. The visual imagery gives me a greater self-awareness and the oneness of body, mind, and spirit.

The most rewarding part is that you can practice at home and without any special equipment. There is nothing else I know that can build muscle tone, relieve tension, and bring inner peace. Yoga has brought more harmony and happiness to my life.

Why I Write

I write for the freedom of a new beginning with each blank page. Something within tells me to put my thoughts on paper to capture my perception of reality. This passion for writing expands my world, increases my awareness, and lets me share my journey in life with others.

My favorite form of writing is poetry. A poem will touch your heart bring music to your soul and thoughts to your mind.

A Poem

P   Putting thoughts on paper

O   Opening your mind

E   Every word has a meaning

M   Motivating you to write a poem

POEMS OF LIFE

Shape

S Shape your life to share

H How you live shows your true self

A Always speak the truth

P Plan your day to achieve

E Every action makes a difference

What is Love?

Love is a deep feeling from the heart
Love was here from the start
Love never fails and endures forever
Love has the power to heal the world
Love God for He will never fail you!

A Mother

Mothers are warm hugs or a
gentle touch
A word of encouragement on a
stressful day
A voice with wisdom to guide
your way
Mothering is a lifelong
endeavor
Mothers are a gift from God
Thank God for Mothers

Empowering

Enabling us to serve God
Making are lives better
Putting God first
Oh give thanks to God
With God all things are possible
Everyday praise God
Rejoice from His blessings
I can do all things through Christ …
Nothing is too hard for God
God is able

Wisdom

Walking by faith
Inspired by His love
Seeking His guidance through prayer
Devoted to studying His word
Obedient to His instructions
Mindful of His blessings

Pray

P Pray each day
R Revitalize your spirit
A Acknowledge his grace
Y You are blessed by his love

Heavenly Father

I come to you with humble
heart
Browed head and closed eyes
Thanking you for all you have
done
I am asking you to bless the
ones I love
Protecting them from all hurt
and harm
Help me to live so others can
see you in me
I praise you for all you have
done
In Jesus name I pray

Someone Knows Your Name

God has a Blessing with your name on it

Matthew 1:20-22

You are eyes that can see a sunset

Ears that can hear the birds sing

A nose that can smell the flowers

A mouth with a voice that can speak

A tongue that can taste different flavors

Fingers that can turn the pages of a book

A body that can feel the touch of a gentle breeze A

heart with love that can reach the heart of others

My name is who I am and God knows my name

What's in a Name?

It is the first thing someone learns about you

It says who you are!

Adam   Eve   Abraham
Sara   Joseph   Muhammad Ali
Malcolm   Rosa Parks
Martin Luther King   Oprah Winfrey
Barack   Michelle   Charles
Martha   Marcella   Charlotte   Henrietta
Cynthia   Mollie
Victoria

Alberta

A Appreciate who I am

L Looks to God for guidance

B Believes in the golden rule

E Enjoys, reading and writing

R Ready to laugh and hear laughter

T Talkative, thoughtful and thankful

A Achieves by striving for excellence!

James

J   Jams to his own tune

A   Adventurous, seeking new ideas

M   Manages to accomplish his goals

E   Enriches the lives of others each day

S   Stands fast on his beliefs

Virginia

V   Very versatile and vibrate

I   Is always doing her best

R   Resourceful radiant and reliable

G   Going for the gold in her golden years

I   Inspiring to those around her

N   Never passing up a chance to help others

I   Is content to live one day at a time

A   Able to achieve her goal

Teddy

T Trusting, truthful and terrific

E Enjoys making people laugh

D Different, daring and dynamite

D Dreams to make things happen

Y You are a rare, unique soul

Mary

Mary is a ray of sun light

An answer to a darken sky

Rarely does she fail to delight

Yet never wonders the reason why

Della

D - Dares to be different

E - Enjoys what she does

L - Luck, left-handed, Libra

L - Lively, Likeable, Lady

A - Achieves by believing in herself

About the Author

Alberta Harvey

Alberta was born one of twelve children to Fred and Tressie Ford and grew up on a small farm in Sullivan, Indiana. She graduated from Sullivan High School, joined the Army, married Roy Harvey, and had a daughter Beverly. Her military training was in the medical field so she continued her education in health care getting and Associate Degree in Nursing from Pikes Peak Community College in Colorado, and a Bachelor of Health Science from Chapman University in California. Her career was in nursing but her real passion was always writing. Writing gives her a new beginning with each blank page. Putting her thoughts on paper increases her awareness and allows her to share them with others…

www.ingramcontent.com/pod-product-compliance
Lightning Source LLC
Chambersburg PA
CBHW031301290426
44109CB00012B/673